THE ASYLUM DANCE

THE ASYLUM DANCE

John Burnside

CAPE POETRY

Published by Jonathan Cape 2000

2 4 6 8 10 9 7 5 3 1

First published in Great Britain in 2000 by
Jonathan Cape
Random House, 20 Vauxhall Bridge Road,
London SW1V 2SA

Random House Australia (Pty) Limited
20 Alfred Street, Milsons Point, Sydney,
New South Wales 2061, Australia

Random House New Zealand Limited
18 Poland Road, Glenfield,
Auckland 10, New Zealand

Random House (Pty) Limited
Endulini, 5A Jubilee Road, Parktown 2193, South Africa

The Random House Group Limited Reg. No. 954009

A CIP catalogue record for this book
is available from the British Library

ISBN 0 224 05938 6

Papers used by The Random House Group Limited are natural,
recyclable products made from wood grown in sustainable forests;
the manufacturing processes conform to the environmental
regulations of the country of origin

Typeset by Palimpsest Book Production Limited,
Polmont, Stirlingshire
Printed and bound in Great Britain by
Creative Print and Design (Wales), Ebbw Vale

for Robin Robertson

The proper dwelling plight lies in this, that mortals ever search anew for the essence of dwelling, that they *must ever learn to dwell*. What if man's homelessness consisted in this, that man still does not even think of the *proper* plight of dwelling as *the* plight? Yet as soon as man *gives thought* to his homelessness, it is a misery no longer. Rightly considered and kept well in mind, it is the sole summons that *calls* mortals into their dwelling.

Heidegger

like the lines in the mane of
a Parthenon horse,
round which the arms had
wound themselves as if they knew love
is the only fortress
strong enough to trust to.

Marianne Moore

CONTENTS

ACKNOWLEDGEMENTS

Acknowledgements are due to the editors of the following:

London Review of Books, New Writing 9, PN Review, Salt, Tabla, and *The Times Literary Supplement.*

The poem 'Sense Data' was commissioned by the Portsmouth City Council for the Shock Waves Festival in 1998.

'The Unprovable Fact: A Tayside Inventory' was commissioned by Dundee Contemporary Arts, as part of an artist and poet collaboration with Will Maclean.

PORTS

'*Pas de port. Ports inconnus.*'
Henri Michaux

I HAVEN

Our dwelling place:
        the light above the firth
shipping forecasts
      gossip
        theorems

the choice of a single word to describe
the gun-metal grey of the sky
           as the gulls
flicker between the roofs
on Tolbooth Wynd.

        Whenever we think of home
we come to this:
the handful of birds and plants we know by name
rain on the fishmonger's window
          the walleyed plaice
freckled with spots
      the colour of orangeade.

We look for the sifted light
that settles around the salvaged
hull of the *Research*
        perched on its metal stocks
by the harbour wall

its smashed keel half-restored
        the workmen

caged in a narrow scaffold
                              matching the ghosts
of umber and *blanc-de-Chine.*

We notice how dark it is
                         a dwelling place
for something in ourselves that understands

the beauty of wreckage
                         the beauty
of things submerged

II URLICHT

                    − our
dwelling place:
                    a catalogue of wrecks
and slants of light −

never the farmsteader's vision
of angels
              his wayside shrines
to martyrs and recent saints
                              the rain
gleaming on wrapped chrysanthemums
                                        forced
roses and pinks −

here we have nothing to go on
                              or nothing more
than light and fog
                    a shiver in the wind
or how the sky can empty all at once
when something like music comes
                              or rather

something like the gap between a sound
and silence
                    like the ceasing of a bell

or like the noise a tank makes as it fills
and overflows.

                    How everyone expects
that moment when a borrowed motor stalls
half-way across the channel
                                        and you sit
quiet
        amazed by the light
                                aware
of everything
                    aware of shoals and stars
shifting around you
                        endlessly

entwined.
                Our neighbour
                        John
who spends his free time diving

plumbing the sea for evidence and spilt
cargoes
            who has burrowed in the mud
to touch the mystery of something absolute

can tell you how
                        out in the Falklands
he walked inland
climbing a slope where blown sand turned to grass
the emptiness over his head
like a form of song.

He still has the pictures he took
                              of backward glances
of whale bones on the shore
                              the wind exact
and plaintive in the whited vertebrae.

He'd been out diving
                              finding the shallow wrecks
of coalships from Wales
                              and one old German
sail-boat
          whose quick-thinking crew
had scuppered it just offshore
to douse a fire:

a cargo of beer and gunpowder
still in the hold
each stoppered bottle
sealed with water weed.

                    He'd walked less than a mile
when
      settled upon its haunches
                              as if it had recently
stopped to rest

he found a carcass: one of those feral
cattle that wander the dunes
                              a long-forgotten
ghost of husbandry.

It might have been there for years
                              but it looked alive
the way it had been preserved
in the cold dry air

4

and he stood in the wind to listen
                                    as if he might hear
radio in the horns
                    or ancient voices
hanging in the vacuum of the skull.

He had his camera
                    but couldn't take
the picture he wanted
                        the one he thinks of now
as perfect
            – he couldn't betray
that animal silence
                    the threadwork of grass through the hide
the dwelling place
                    inherent in the spine

                                    that

III MOORINGS

kinship of flesh with flesh.

                            When we go walking
early
        at the furled edge of the sea

we find dark webs of crabmeat
                                    herring-bone
                                                wet
diaphragms of stranded jellyfish

spring water mingles with salt beneath the church
where Anstruther's dead are harboured in silent loam

sea–litter washes the wall where the graveyard ends
a scatter of shells and hairweed

                      and pebbles of glass
made smooth
          in the sway of the tide.

From here
         amongst the angel–headed stones
we see the town entire:
            the shiplike kirk
the snooker hall above the library

the gift–shop on the corner
               windows packed
with trinkets of glass
          and pictures of towns like this

a rabble of gulls
         the scarlet and cherry red
of lifebelts and cars
          the bus that will wait by the dock
for minutes
        before it returns
to Leven.

      By evening the harbour belongs
to men at work.
They're swaddled in orange or lime–green
overalls
     their faces sheathed
in perspex: crouched to the blue
of their torches
        they are innocent
of presence
       flashes and sparks

dancing in the blackness of their masks
as if in emptiness.

Sometimes we stand in the cold
and watch them for hours
                              – the way
they bend into their flames
like celebrants
                    immune to everything
that moves or falls around them
                                        isolates
suspended in the constancy
of fire.
            This time of year
it's night by five o'clock
and as we walk
                  we harbour something new:
                                          the old pain
neutral and stilled in our blood
like a shipwreck observed from a distance
                                          or one of those
underwater shapes we sometimes glimpse
through hairweed and clouded sand
                  a shifting form
that catches the eye for a moment
then disappears.

At dusk
            above the street
                              above the painted
shopfronts and roofs
and children walking home in twos and threes
it starts to snow.
                  At one end of the quay
a boat is docked

– it's mostly fishing vessels here
                                    but this
is tusk–white
                    with a terracotta keel
a pleasure boat
                    a hope pursued through years
of casual loss.

It's unattended now
                    but you could guess
its owner from the writing on the hull
a stencilled row of characters that spell
against the painted wood
                                    the word
S E R E N I T Y.

In daylight it would seem
almost absurd:
too sentimental
                    gauche
                                    inaccurate
a weekend sailor's image of the sea

but now
            as snow descends into the rings
of torchlight
                    and the sky above the harbour
darkens
            it is only what it seems:

a name for something wanted
                                    and believed

no more or less correct than anything
we use to make a dwelling in the world.

GEESE

It happens every time.
We wonder about the geese
on our drive to work –
        passing the ferry
or slowing amongst the fields
of water and reeds –

and they come
        out of nowhere
resuming the game they will make
of distance.

It's reassuring then
        to think
that anything could be
so punctual and loud
their voices splashing in the sky
above us
        and the bodies surging on
towards the light.

In school
        we were taught to admire
the homing instinct
        animate and sharp
behind the eyes
ignoring this vast delight
        this useless motion.

I'd think of them gorged on savannah
        or native corn
an African heat laid down
        in the well-oiled feathers
or mingling with salt and berries
        in the blood.

I'd think of tundra
          birchwoods under snow
hectares of lake and ozone
          and the odd
glimmer of random light
amongst the trees

but I couldn't imagine the maps
by which they travelled:
          miles of surface
etched into the brain's
          wet geometry.

I couldn't imagine
          the pull and sway of home
unless it was play they intended:
          that no good reason
of purposed joy.

Round here
          they mostly arrive
in sixes and sevens
dropping to rest for a time
          at the edge of the firth
then moving on

          but once
in the first grey of morning
          travelling north
I saw them in their hundreds:
          one broad
wave of black and white
          the motion
verging on standstill.

I parked the car
        and stepped out
to the rush of it:
a rhythm I had waited years
to feel in the meat of my spine
        and the bones of my face

and a long time after they passed
I could feel it still:
not what my teachers had seen
        that mechanical
flicker of instinct
nothing magnetic
        no skill
and no sense of direction

but homing
        in the purer urgency
of elsewhere
        which is nothing like the mind's
intended space
        but how the flesh belongs.

SENSE DATA

John Goodricke, (1764–1786)

We measured things for years: our schoolroom walls,
the growth of plants, lost energy, shed skins.

We counted petals, tadpoles, grains of sand,
observed migrations, rainfalls, frequencies.

I thought there was a chromatography
for happiness, or unrequited love,

and somewhere behind it all, in private realms
of gulls' eggs and stones and things I couldn't name,

another world of charge and borderline,
an earth-tide in the spine, the nightlong
guesswork of old voices in the mind.

Waking at night, I would sneak downstairs in the dark
and know my way by some unconscious craft,

some seventh sense that recognised
a deeper pulse, the tug of things at rest,

the tension in a table, or a vase
of goldenrod
            – and when I stood outside,

head tilted to a night-sky packed with light
I waited for a music I could feel

like motion in the marrow of my bones,
as Goodricke must have done, night after night,

beyond all hearing, resonant as some
struck bell, harmonics
singing in his blood,

his fingertips and eyelids bruised with grace
and tuned into the plainsong of the stars.

A prostitute, in fact.

                    We know this
by the rush mat under her arm
                              and by the way
her sash is tied.

The snow has been falling all day
in thick
        slow
              waves

filling the gaps between the young bamboos

blurring the lanternlight behind her with a scuffed
white fur.

            She must be cold:
she is shielding her face from the wind
and her feet are naked in the high
wood sandals
              which leave a trail
of blue-black chevrons on the narrow path
like crow's-feet
                or the blocked calligraphy
that hides an artist's name and printer's mark

amongst the grey-green spikes
of winter leaves.

BLUES

It's moments like this
      when the barman goes through the back
and leaves me alone

a radio whispering
      somewhere amongst the glasses
– *I'm through with love* –

the way the traffic slows
      to nothing
how all of a sudden
      at three in the afternoon

the evening's already begun
      a nascent
dimming.

      By ten I'll be walking away
on Union Street
      or crossing Commercial Road
in a gust of rain

  and everyone who passes
      will be you
or almost you
      before it's someone else.

II

or how I feel tonight
    abandoned
                stilled
aware of every nerve
    of every

pin-point of fatigue
    and nursed assent
encrypted angels
    dangling in the blood
acidic singularities
    of fire.

The way I am emptied
    for every
and no good reason
becalmed and absurdly
    expert in the art
of boiling a kettle
    or raising a cup
to my mouth

like the night I'd been travelling
    for hours
on a slow-moving train:
snow on the open fields
    the whiteness
glimmering
    mile after mile
                like a child's

impression of infinity
        – the odd
wavering bend in the road
        and a single
mint–coloured lamp for gas
        or a roadside bar.

I was halfway to sleep
or perhaps I had slept
        unawares
then started awake
when the train pulled
        into the station
and didn't move on

and though I was waiting to ask
        no one came to explain
and I sat there for hours
with my face
        to the ice–cold glass

the windows half reflection
                half
some vaguely good–humoured
        notion of dissolve

the place–name on the signpost
        almost gone
some local or native word
        for 'hopelessly lost'

III

or how I keep thinking of nowhere
        and meaning you
— spaces you might inhabit
        as the light

inhabits doors
        or windows
                        or the bright
membrane of yolk and milk
on the kitchen table —

the way a sound
        — this music
                        or the owls'
nightlong to and fro
        of lulls and cries —

rests in the mind for years
        like a childhood dream
whatever remains unfinished:
        the not-pursued
each glimmer on the cusp
        of touch
                or loss.

DESSERTS

and afterwards
                    travelling home
on the northbound train
my body is wired
                    to the flavours
of childhood:
                    aniseed
and mint
          and something sharp
or incompletely sweetened
                         like the stalks
of rhubarb we would cut from old
allotments
          dipped
in stolen sugar
               reddled at the lips
and trying to imagine nights like this:
a butterkist warmth on my tongue
                              and the craquelure
of egg-yolk
          and cream of the well
on the maze of your skin.

ADAM AND EVE

I always think of them
as innocents:
too much intended for sin
                    they walk their garden
stunned with a local wonder
                         angels and beasts
inured to everything but them
or lost in unwitting joy
like the dreamed unborn.

                  Imagine that first
cold morning: frosted grass
and fruit-falls running to black
amongst the leaves
the meadows they had laced with given names
muffled in snow
              the net of birdsong
gone.

    We get what we least expect
and most require
was all the explanation I received
in scripture class
             the serpent in the weeds
named from the start
               the stillness of each blizzard
preordained.

Imagine them surrendering to white
as we do
        when the snow begins again
falling from nowhere on James Street
                    then crossing the park

to discover the kirk
                like a song
                              or a prayer learned by heart

or all those games of tag
and catch-kiss that we never quite
abandoned
               children
wandering off to the furthest
corners of a snowfall
                   calling
softly from street to street
                        their half-goodbyes
but never imagining this:
                      the sudden halt
between the baker's and the library
lights coming on in houses and crowded shops
the quick wind sealing us in
                        or a snowbound silence
fading us out.

              I always think of them
as innocents
             with something more to learn
much like ourselves when we come to this
surprise:
             our bodies
half-inhabited

and finding it harder to live
with others:
             with each new winter
                     each new space
the gardens we remember in our sleep

filling with snow all day

                        as we come to require

this white-out

           this
sufficiency of names.

SETTLEMENTS

'God answers our prayers by refusing them.'
Luther

I A PLACE BY THE SEA

Because what we think of as home
is a hazard to others
our shorelines edged with rocks and shallow
sandbanks
      reefs
where navigation fails

we mark the harbour out
with lights and noise:
flickers of green and scarlet in the dark
the long moan of a foghorn
                 when the daylight
thickens and stills

and even when we speak of other things
our prayers include all ships
            all those at sea
navigators   pilots   lobster-crews
the man who is yanked overboard
on a line of creels
whole families of boys and quiet fathers
lost in a sudden squall
           a mile from land.

It's not that we surrender to our fear
or trust in nothing
it's just that the darkness
opens
      on mornings like this

filling with distance and starlight for mile after mile
when we wake to the taste of milk
                                    and the scent of coal
in rooms bequeathed to us by merchantmen
who stocked the roof with powders
                                    sacks of grain
spicetree and crumbs of saffron

it's not that we are lost
or far from home

it's just that the world
seems strange
            on nights like this

when we lie with the ghosts of ourselves
                                    – these habitual flavours:
aloe and eau-de-cologne
                        and the ribbon of sweetness
that stays on my hands for hours
when I turn
            to sleep

II FISHERFOLK AT NEWHAVEN
after Hill and Adamson

Mending their nets
                        or standing in their dim
smoke houses
                hearing the water
slap against the wood-face of the dock

and thinking of nights at sea
                              of a spilt
quiver of brindled fish
on the slur of the deck

of calling back and forth through lanternlight
for uncles and second cousins
to come and look:

the fruits of the ocean
                              tarred with a difficult blue
as they haul them in
siren faces poised
                    as if to speak

but silent
          like the wives they leave behind
for weeks and months
                              beguiled by the wounded skins
they bring in from the dark
                              the slatted crates

dripping with salt and copper
                              and the pale
shimmer of phosphorescence
                              like the chill
that grows between their hands
                              on chapel days.

III WELL

There's more to it than I thought –
more than the house, or our stilled bed
when no one is here,

25

the book you have left face down
on the kitchen table,
the tangle of hair in the brush, the litter of clothes
– there's more to the making of home
than I ever expected:
a process of excavation, of finding
something in myself to set against
the chill of the other,
the echo you do not hear, when I stop to listen,
the stranger who wakes in the dark from a fetid dream
of ditches and milt;
and how we go on digging when it seems
there's nothing else to find – or nothing more
than ghosts and unanswered prayers –
is part of it, though not the better part
we hoped for: it's the old need
keeps us strong.
So when I turn to say, at times like this,
that something else is with us all along
I'm thinking of that woman in the town
who told me how she worked all afternoon,
she and her husband digging in the heat, bees
drifting back and forth through currant stands,
the sound of their breathing
meshed with the weave and spin
of swallows:
how, after an hour, they struck on an unexpected
flagstone of granite
and lifted the lid on a coal-black
circle of fresh spring water under the stone,
leaning in hard for the earth-smell of last year's fruit
then sweetness, surprising as rain, or bittern-calls,
rising like a slow, unfurling shoot
of asphodel.
                    It's what I think of now

as home: that wellspring
deep beneath the house
they tasted for an hour, then put away,
sliding the cover back, and coming in
to all they knew, immersed in the quiet purr
of radio, those voices from the air
bleeding in through swallow-songs and bees
to make them plausible again, though they had touched
what turns to black; the sifted heart of matter.

IV WHAT WE KNOW OF HOUSES

Sunday
        We are driving to the woods
to find the hidden origin of rain:
a shallow basin carved into the rock
where Pictish chiefs assembled with their kin
to reinvent the world
                        – or so we say –
though no one knows for sure who gathered here
or why.

        I like to think of them
on days like this
perched on a shelf of rock beneath the trees
watching their children
                        thinking of their stock
then stepping out
                to sacrifice
                        or blessing
as we have stood together in the shade
made awkward by the quiet of the place
a darkness that continues while the sun
brightens the fields

and gardens fill with light
in market towns or tidy golf-hotels
above the sea.

Though nothing here is sacred
                              – not to us –
even the pool of water stopped with leaves
the carvings in the rock
                         the standing stone
are set apart

and nothing we can touch or say will bring us
closer to the spirit of the place.
Our holy ground is barely recognised:
unverified
            an atmospheric trick
a common miracle that finds us out
alone in attic rooms
                      as spring begins:
a rhythm in the light
                        a line of song
the sudden taste of grass
                           high in the roof
wind through the gaps in the beams
                                 the rafters spiced
with cumin
and the aftertaste of nets

and all along the roads
                        where dry-stone walls
have toppled
            and the steady gorse digs in
embers of perfume, sealed in a crown of thorns:

unseasonable   stubborn   everyday

– it's bright as the notion of home:

                                    not something held
or given
            but the painful gravity
that comes of being settled on the earth
redeemable   inventive   inexact
and capable of holding what we love
in common
                    making good
with work and celebration
                                    charged
to go out unprepared into the world

and take our place for granted
                                    every time
we drive back through the slowly dimming fields
to quiet rooms
                    and prayers that stay unanswered.

ARRIVAL OF THE MAIL BOAT

after Edvard Munch

It takes us years to understand
the colours of perpetual return:
grey-green on the pier; the blue of shadows;
smoke over water, or flight, or an angler's
baffled reflection;

that red in the distance – a flag,
or a woman's dress –
passing for the irretrievable;
those promised letters, cleaner and more precise
than any we ever received, in days gone by,

still in the hold, like birds, or the quiet folds
of bridal dresses, sailcloth, reams of salt.

THE ASYLUM DANCE

for Dag Andersson

At one time, I looked forward to the dance:
wandering back and forth in the quiet
heat of an August morning,
packing the car with cup cakes and lemonade,
boxes of plums or cherries, petits-fours,
nuts and spice cake, mousse and vol-au-vents.
At noon I would go upstairs
to wash and change
– Sunday best, a clean white shirt and tie –
while mother made her face
and fixed her hair.
It was something we did, every year,
in that backwater town,
abandoning our lawns and flower beds,
to meet the patients, out at Summerswood.
It seemed a privilege to be allowed
within those gates, and know we might return,
to see the meadows, striped with light and shade,
the silent lake, the fallen cedar trees.
We went there for the dance: a ritual
of touch and distance, webs of courtesy
and guesswork; shifts
from sunlight into shade;
and when the patients came downstairs
to join us, smiling, utterly polite,
in new-pressed clothes, like cousins twice-removed,
they had the look of people glimpsed in mirrors,
subtle as ghosts, yet real, with the vague
good-humour of the lost.
How we appeared to them, I can only imagine:

too solid, perhaps, too easy with ourselves,
sure of our movements, blessed with a measured desire.
All afternoon we picnicked on the lawn
then danced in awkward couples to the hiss
of gramophones, as daylight turned to dusk;
a subtle exchange in the half-light; acts of grace:
townsfolk conferring the weight of a normal world,
homes in the suburbs, the brisk lives of men who can who sleep,
the practised charm of women who believe,
who wake and forget what they dreamed, and go off to work,
and wish for nothing.
Beside the patients, we were lithe and calm:
we doled out charity and easy praise
and waited for the dancing to erase
the pain in the knot of the throat, the birdlike
angle of defeat against the spine.
We loved them for the way they witnessed us,
standing in twos and threes in the waning light,
made other by the rhythm of the dance,
the pull of a larger world, and that taste on the air
of birch-woods and streams: that knowledge of ourselves
as bodies clothed in brightness, moving apart
and coming together, cooling
slowly, as the lawns and rose-beds cooled,
heat seeping out from the skin and bleeding away,
the goldenrod turning to smoke
at the fence line.
Friendships began out there, to be resumed
year after year, the difficult months between
absolved by the summer light; and once,
a love affair, of sorts: an awkward boy
finding a girl, and leading her, mock-unwilling
into the lighted circle of the dance, to venture steps
that felt like steps on ice, the floorboards

creaking, and thin as paper.
They danced less than an hour, then she was gone,
and when he went back, next morning, the nurses
turned him away.
I think of her every day, I dream her skin,
and for years I have driven out, in the August heat,
alone now, with Mother gone, and my contributions
store-bought: jars of pickles; cling-wrapped bread.
I stand by myself, excused from the solid ring
of bodies and, for minutes at a time,
I see it all from somewhere far above,
some landing in the house, some upper room:
it makes me think of pictures I have seen
of dancers – wisps of movement on a lawn
at sunset: faces muffled, bodies twined;
the figures so close to the darkness, they might be
apparitions, venturing on form,
pinewoods above the lake, a suggestion of watchers,
a gap between night and day, between light and shade,
and faces melting, one into the next
as if they were all one flesh, in a single dream,
and nothing to make them true, but space, and time.

THE DANCE OF LIFE

after Edvard Munch

It's the summer we'll never reach:
                              the final
arrangement of bodies.
                              Flesh
given to the air
                  becoming light
                              or evening
or the memory of rain

as grass is.
            It's the habitable place
we make
        not of death
              or absence
                        but of how
the dancers move together
                        to become
these disappearances.
                      No aftermath or stain
though somewhere across the lake
                              amongst the rocks
where someone has hauled an upturned boat ashore
– the white of the hull in the moonlight
like a sign –
their conversation carries on the wind:
promises
        lies
              and the rhythms we've come to expect
from the painted dark.

FIELDS

*'From my rotting body, flowers shall grow and I am in them
and that is eternity.'*

Edvard Munch

I LANDFILL

In ways the dead are placed
                              or how
they come to rest

I recognise myself
                    insomniac
                              arms
angled
      or crossed:

children in skullcaps
soldiers with hob-nailed boots
or sandals placed like gifts
beside their feet

priests at the gates of death
                              or afterlife
their vestments stained with malt
and carbon
           fingers rinsed
with camomile
              or honeyed meadowsweet

resemble me
           laid sleepless by your side
as if there were something else
                                some chore or rite
to be accomplished.
                    Once

35

in rural Fife
   and Angus
      farmers held
one acre of their land
     untilled
       unscarred
to house this mute
concurrence with the dead
choosing from all their fields
one empty plot
that smelled or tasted right
        one house of dreams.

They walled it in
and called it Gude Man's Land
      or Devil's Piece

and some would say they guessed well every time
knowing the gist of the thing
       the black in the green
of stitchwort.
     Though I can't believe they thought
that tremor in the grass on windless days
was devil's work:
     yet
where they found old bones
       or spills of blood
where birdsong ceased
and darkness stayed till noon
they recognised some kinship with the dead
with bodies they had found
       in nether fields
the faces soft
    still lifelike
      grass and roots

decaying in the gut.
They guessed it well
                    divined its mysteries
and left it to the pipistrelles
and jays.

When I was five
or six
        – I can't recall –
the land for miles was sick with foot and mouth

and grateful for the work
                          my father
travelled the length of the county
                                    digging pits
for slaughtered herds.

On farm after farm for miles
                              in the paling light
he worked all day
                  and far into the dusk
then caught the last bus home
                              his shirtsleeves stitched
with quicklime and dust.

That was the year our neighbour
                                Agnes
                                      died:
her body thick with growth
                          the blackness
tight between her lips
like needlework.

I thought she had been touched by foot and mouth:
a fog of disease that spread

on our spoons and knives
and bottles in the playground
stopped with cream

and I waited for my father to begin
unravelling
like twine.

I stood in the kitchen and watched
while my mother
fixed him his tea
amazed at how lonely he looked
how suddenly tired
a blur of unspoken hurt
on his mouth and eyes

and I loitered all afternoon
while friends and strangers
emptied the house our neighbour had kept intact
and still as a church.

They worked all day
intent and businesslike
clearing the rooms
the wardrobes
the silent cupboards
folding her winter coats and summer shawls
packing her shoes in boxes
her letters
her make-up
and bearing it away
to other rooms
timesoiled
infected.

I scarcely recall:
                    there was something I overheard
a sense of the ditch
                         and the blind calves laid in the earth
a nightmare for weeks
of gunshots
               and buried flesh

yet still
          when I lie naked in our bed
I sense my father waiting
                         and I shift
like someone in a dream
                         so he will turn
and go back to the fire
                         and let me rest.

II TWO GARDENS

When we came it was couch-grass and brambles,
colonies of rue amongst the thorns,
a leafless shrub that smelt of creosote
and simmered in the heat.
I liked it then. I liked its stillnesses:
the ruined glasshouse packed with honey-vine,
the veins of ash, the pools of fetid rain.
Sometimes we found strange droppings by the hedge:
badger or fox, you said; but the scent was laced
with citrus, and I kept imagining
a soft-boned creature stalled beneath the shed,
strayed from its purpose, wrapped in musk and spines.
In spring we set to work; we marked our bounds
and found the blueprint hidden in the weeds,
implicit beds, the notion of a pond.
You sifted out the shards of porcelain,

39

illumined willows, scraps of crescent moon;
I gathered clinker, labels, half a set
of Lego.
          As I watched that summer's fires
I wondered what was burning: living bone,
pockets of silk and resin, eggs and spawn,
and, afterwards, I saw what we had lost:
surrendered to our use, inanimate,
the land was measured out in bricks and twine,
a barbecue, a limestone patio.
The work is finished now; but after dark
I feel the creatures shivering away,
abandoning an absence we accept
as natural: the unexpectant trees;
the silence where the blackbird vanishes.
At times the ghosts are almost visible
between our trellises and folding chairs:
just as old harbours sometimes reappear
through fog or rain, or market towns dissolve
to gift us with a dusk of shining air,
the garden we destroyed is almost here,
nothing but hints and traces, nothing known,
but something I have wanted all along:
a thread of pitchblende, bleeding through a stone,
or snow all morning, cancelling the lawn.

III GUDE MAN'S LAND

There was something I wanted to find,
coming home late in the dark, my fingers
studded with clay,
oak-flowers caught in my hair, the folds of my jacket
busy with aphids.
I slept in my working clothes

and walked out in the buttermilk of dawn
to start again.
Sometimes I turned and saw him through the leaves,
a face like mine, but empty of desire,
pure mockery, precision of intent,
a poacher's guile, a butcher's casual charm.
The house filled slowly with the evidence
I carried home: old metals, twisted roots,
bottles of silt and water, scraps of cloth.
My neighbours passed me on the road to kirk
and thought me mad, no doubt, though I could see
their omnipresent God was neither
here nor there.
Who blurred the sheep with scab? Who curdled milk?
Who was it fledged the wombs of speechless girls?
They knew, and made their standard offerings
and called it peace. But he was with them still.
His secret thoughts were written in their veins,
and when they dreamed of music, it was his,
and when I dreamed, I fed him in the dark,
wifeless and quiet, lacking in conversation.
He knew what I wanted; I knew what I would not dare;
lying alone in the darkness, burning with fever,
walking the fields in the rain, at home and lost,
the feel of his recent warmth
on the tips of my fingers,
the taste of his body minted in the wild
patches of grass that quickened along the walls
or ran in circles round the nether field,
absorbing the daylight,
informing the guesswork of children.

Be quick when you switch on the light
and you'll see the dark
was how my father put it:
                              catch
the otherlife of things
                         before a look
immerses them.
                  Be quick
and you'll see the devil at your back
and he'd grin
                as he stood in the garden
– cleaning his mower
                       wiping each blade in turn
with a cotton rag
the pulped grass and bright–green liquor
staining his thumbnails
and knuckles.
                He always seemed
transfigured by the work
glad of his body's warmth
                           and the smell
of aftermath.
He'd smoke behind the shed
                            or dart
for shelter under the eaves
                             the fag-end
cradled in his hand
against the rain:

a man in an old white shirt
                             a pair of jeans
some workboots he'd bought for a job
that was never completed.
                           And later
                                     after he died

I buried those clothes in a field above the town
finding a disused lair amongst the stones
that tasted of water
                    then moss
                              then something
sharper
        like a struck match in the grass
or how he once had smelled
                              home from the pit
his body doused in gas
                    and anthracite.

I still remember
                somewhere in the flesh
asleep and waking
                how the body looked
that I had made
the empty shirt and jeans
                        the hobnailed boots
and how I sat for hours
                    in that wet den
where something should have changed
                                as skin and bone
are altered
        and a new life burrows free
– sloughed from a slurry of egg-yolk
                                or matted leaves
gifted with absence
                speaking a different tongue –
but all I found in there was mould and spoor
where something had crept away
                            to feed
                                or die
or all I can tell
                though for years I have sat up late

43

and thought of something more
                              some half-seen thing
the pull of the withheld
                        the foreign joy
I tasted that one afternoon
                        and left behind
when I made my way back down the hill
with the known world about me.

BLUE

The way some towns would change under a rain
in childhood
and how they no longer do, or are never quite
as blue as they were: the windows turning to dusk
in the seafront cafe
and stairwells filling quickly with a thick
damp fur.
            The way we found ourselves
in waiting rooms and haberdashers' shops
gone strange in the blue of it: fish-scaled, with souls of ink;
the way we stood for hours
in the town museum,
watching that bowl of cinquecento fruit
the painter had sickened with rot – the one thing we knew
in all that gold and amber, perfect scabs
of blue-black mottling the skin
and haunted by the memory
of flies;
            and how, in snow-light, walking home from Mass
we chose it over incense and the singing
dizziness that made us think of God,
stepping away from the crib and the noise of bells
to feel the midnight darkness from the woods
cooling our faces, pagan and undefiled.

THE HAY DEVIL

I

Where logic seems apparent:
in bullfrogs
      or Black-Eyed Susans
bird migrations
         patterns on the skin
of newt or carp

we go too far
        imagining a god
of purposes.
        Where vanity or sense
is satisfied
where beauty is symmetrical
           or lit
by something inward
        where we meet ourselves
by other ways and means
we call it order.
        Even tidal waves
and falls of ash
become mathematical
        equations
stitched into the seams of space and time.
Or so you said.
        I hadn't thought of it
till then
wanting no more than home
and a sense of direction
a named world
        with its space for mystery
perfect and still
      like shale
        or the sleep between dreams

but one day
        driving back from open plain
we saw a drift of grass above a field
and felt the motion echo in our spines
like waves of song.
               It came as a surprise:
the slow afternoons and miles to the nearest horizon
had lulled me into a sense
that nothing could happen here
                    or nothing much
that couldn't be foreseen: heat-shimmer
                       rain
the tidal grasslands shifting through a range
of reds and golds.
            I'd seen those grainy films
of sixties children chasing wisps of hay
as if they would be lifted from a ring
of warmth and noise and rise into the chill
of sky.
        I knew the explanation for this strange
phenomenon
           but hadn't guessed till then
how sweet it is: almost to disappear
rising a little
        or flaring towards the light
with every spinning clutch
of windblown grass

and later
      in the uneventful dusk
we drove out to a field beyond the town
and wandered the riverbank
                    searching for a spill
of osage orange: gold skins seamed and ridged
like child-sized brains.
                 You wanted me to see
the chaos in the rind
            the disarray
the beauty of it
       asymmetrical
and useless
      like the Taoist master's tree
that grew awry
        too gnarled and dense to cut
for lumber.

A breeze was blowing through the cottonwoods
and on our way home the streets were fuzzed and blurred
with drifted hay
       familiar alleys dim
and mazy.
      I had carried back a fruit
holding it like some animal between
my cradled hands
        as if it might be hurt
by contact.
      There was something in its weight
that seemed alive
       a warmed magnetic force
that bled into my fingers like a pulse
and it was days

before I threw it out
                        the seams decayed
and crumpled
                flesh diseased
with patient rot.

IV

Now I am back
and home is a different country:
eel-streams in the fields
                          the narrow woods
a calm between the hills
that might be rain.
Home is a reason
                a word from a children's primer
the field I have crossed today
for the hundredth time:
the sway of the wind in my hands
and a pulse in my spine
and something in the distance
                                    shoreline
                                              firth
a wreath of smoke above the paper mill
fruit farms
            the taste of salt
                        a string of birds
the sudden hiatus of stubble
                              or tidewashed sand
from the same dream
                    year after year:
in autumn
          when the crops are gathered in
a man sets out to cross a field of grain
and somewhere along the way he disappears
turning to something else
                          the wind
                                    the light
not vanishing
              but ceasing to exist
gone into becoming
                  reattuned
to some pure rhythm written on the air.

If things happened the way they said
in bible school
an angel at the door
                    the soul
white as a new-laundered shirt
                              the body
discarded
          or laid to rest
amongst bloodroot and corms
it's the journeys we make
                    you said
                              not our sins
that we have to account for:
places we passed on a road
                    and failed
to recognise:
the light in a gap between trees
that we barely noticed
storms above a hayfield
                    like the black
in monochrome
                    the neither here nor there
of detours
          or oncoming traffic.
It's the lives we failed to lead
lost in a stalled conversation
                              or glancing away
to cottonwoods
                    and miles of blue-stemmed grass
and everything we miss
                    each least detail
patterns and lines in the packed
silt around a mooring
                    windows
flecked with light and water
                              shades of grey
in this
          or any other afternoon.

V

                         And now
this evening's sky:
the seep of cloud through cloud so black
it looks like wreaths of ink
unfurled in water
                         dock-lights
spotting the further shore:
                              quicksilver
                                        gold
and crimson
               one white boat
dissolving in the firth.
It's gone before I've seen it: details
changing
          light
imagining a world:
                    the play of wind
and traffic
            voices
                    footsteps on the street
intruding on my thoughts like some
perpetual film of space
                          or coming home
or counting out a lifetime's worth of sails
and other people's gardens smudged with rain
or wisps of drifted hay
                         that catch the light
and vanish
           as I never quite arrive
at absence
           which is presence somewhere else
in some bright field
                     some miracle of air.

HUSBANDRY

Why children make pulp of slugs
with a sprinkling of salt

or hang a nest of fledglings on a gate
with stolen pins

is why I sometimes turn towards the dark
and leave you guessing.

only to know the butter and nickel taste
of cruelty;
             to watch, and show no sign

of having seen
             Not
wickedness, that sometimes celebrates

a tightness in the mind;
but what I comprehend

of fear and love:
cradled remoteness, nurtured by stalled desire;

willed deprivation;
the silence I'm learning by heart.

ARCHAEOLOGY

for Melanie and Kate

Imagine they knew already: a loved one
singled out in permafrost, or sand;
fingertips laying stitch-marks in the skin
that might be read; each
wedding-feast or name-day laying claim
to birth-marks, dimples, curvatures of bone.
Imagine they treasured scars for what they tell
of summers, traces set into the flesh
for August noons; or winter solstices
remembered in a burn. Imagine it:
not loving less, but more, for knowing time
would quietly erase a lover's voice,
a grandchild's hand;
                          and how, unwittingly,
they planned each afterlife, concealing seed
and pollen in the hemline of a gown,
or carving timberwork with hidden signs,
seasons and gifts that someone else would find.

FIDELITY

It's some
    inevitable end
that one house
    echoes another:

settlements and shifts
    behind a door
accumulations
    traces
vacancies.

So when I come in
from work
    and catch you
sleeping in a chair

it's not just you I see
    but someone else
– someone I've never met
    and tried to reach
in every house I knew
    and left behind:

a common ghost
    though
no one you'd expect
no sisterling
    or mother-in-the-green
only the other woman
    who arrives

and goes
    before I know
she's ever there

and isn't you
        can no more take your place
than rainfall
        or some perfume
on the air.

A SMOKE

The harbour's empty of water
                    gulls
wading the sweet mud

as I walk to the shell
of the lighthouse
                    the mineral kiss

of nicotine and tar
between my lips
                    each knot of smoke

fingered by a wind that tastes
of fairgrounds and far-off

dance halls
            and the burn
of exit lights in Perth or Cardenden

pleasures so small
they flicker on my skin

like cheap perfume
or someone else's rain.

THE SINGER

A weekday haar.
                    The boats are out to sea
in a radio stasis, physical and stilled
between the water and unending sky.
It's late in the afternoon; it's holiday:
they've set the fair up at the harbour's edge
amongst the lobster creels and fishing nets,
matching the reds of marker buoys and floats
with scarlet bulbs and candied apple-skins.
The rides look pale and quiet in the grey
of four o'clock, and most are stalled, or vacant,
waiting for the night and mystery.
On days like these the fair is mostly refuge:
the booths at the pier-end lit against the fog
like one of those chalk-coloured prints that Harunobu
committed to paper so fine it seems
intangible, a pop song from the sixties
working against the foghorn's steady bass
like tinselwork.
                    On days like these
the one thing that never ends is the expectancy
of standing in the haar and listening
for stars on their crystal axis, or the slide
of nightfall, like the whisper in the strands
of coloured lights around the carousel.
The singer is lost in a web
of speakers and wires, and voices from the quay,
but now and then she rises through it all,
her voice like a thread I keep
losing and finding again, though I'm never quite sure
if it's love she intends, or loss, or a moment's
angry hosanna.
                    At sea

the stillness thickens, charged with idle boats
and schools of fishes swimming in the blur
of memory, or joy, or what it is
to happen in the hurry of a world
that ebbs and flows like song, or given light,
against the random static of the dark.

THE MEN'S HARBOUR

Late November, Anstruther

The eider are back
              Formal as decoys
they sit at the end of the quay
in the day's first warmth;
Sunday: when the townsmen bring their sons
to fish off the dock,
their rods propped by the wall, the tensed lines
streaming with light;
the boys in hats and scarves and brightly-coloured
anoraks; the men
sober, reflective; wrapped in the quiet of work
that is theirs, for once, and unaccountable

and I can't help but think
there is something they want to pass on:
a knowledge they can't quite voice though it has to do
with the grace that distinguishes strength
from power.
              Beyond the quay,
a crew of gulls is shredding refuse sacks
for morsels of fishbone, choice
oozings of yoghurt or mango.
They half co-operate, half
vie with one another, butting in
for fatter scraps, then fluttering away,
tracking the tarmac with newsprint and crusted grease.

There's nothing elegant in this, no special skill,
nothing save luck and speed and the odd
flutter of threat: a clownish, loud
bravado.

    Further upshore,
the sun finds the white on white
of the caravan park:
blisters of paint and distemper flaking away
from brickwork and metal;
alleys of half-kept garden between the stands;
the scalped grass dusted with frost; a single blackbird
scratching for grubs in the dirt of the island bed.

Someone has set a flag above the dock;
a thin old man in a jerkin and fingerless gloves
mending a hull, his tight lips crammed with nails,
his eyes like shells,
and others here are working on their dreams
of water: men in overalls or coats,
or muddled sweaters, scabbed with paint and rust.
Their hands are dark with oil or coiled in rope;
their bodies subtle, verging on the edge
of weightlessness; no law to hold them here,
no harboured rage.

This is the life they want, their chosen craft,
working with hooks and chains through the sea-water-cold.
Each of them knows what it is
to have been refused,
to feel the silence swelling in their throats
and nothing to be said, lest they admit
how little they care for anything but this,
wanting a life that stays
untraceable.
            Each of them knows
and each of them makes his peace:
the burden of a given name and place
discarded in a moment's self-forgetting.

They're out at the rim of navigable space
and ready for something no one could explain,
a mystery to fathom when it comes
like starlight, or a music in the tide,
or some new vessel, coming in to land,
one cold, bright afternoon: some unknown craft
with snow on the deck, or a phantom of morning lamplight
sealed in the hull's bright paint
like the spirit of tungsten.

KESTREL

'so that my mind would be one selving or pitch of a great universal mind,
working in other minds too besides mine, and even in all other things,
according to their natures and powers'
Gerard Manley Hopkins

We found it at the end of Tollcross Lane
between the garage and that bordeline of hedge
where snows begin
like stories told to children:
one of those cold, bright mornings; seams of frost
arriving through the grass, the dead bird's feathers
perfect as bronze, the narrow raptor's face
all beak and eyes.
You probed it with a stick; it seemed alive,
or haunted with the aftertaste of life;
the tension in the wings; the vivid claws;
the hooded skull a mutant hieroglyph
for sunlight, or transmigration.
This was the god of silence and the sky
in ancient times
and Hopkins' dapple-dawn-drawn
falcon: Christ
and Horus.
So, though I am no believer, I could find
the blue-bleak ember of an old
significance, the promise that remains
unsayable, laid down between the folds
of flesh and blood,
since what we make of gravity, or fire,
infers the soul:
a light that pools and lingers in the mud;
a sunlit field; the wind that stains the plumage
blue-black, and the warmth that flows between

my fingers and the kestrel's emptied frame.
It's what we make of memory and fear
and how each body wills its transformation,
hoarding a fall against the level air,
each thread of breaking fire it cannot hold
surrendered, and lost, for subtleties of gold.

THE UNPROVABLE FACT:
A TAYSIDE INVENTORY

From a distance
    they only missed
what they never saw:
the pull of borderlines
    slow
tide shifts in the angle of a wall
the slip of water
    underneath a quay
shadows that came through snow
    on a journey home.
From a distance they began
    the stories they would use
as camouflage:
ghost companions
    birds beneath their feet
rockfalls
    or the memory of something
lukewarm:
    moths and pollen
hidden in the seams
    of wintered shirts
gardens laid out in rows
    like oyster beds
a house of silverfish
    beyond the docks
the doorway thick with steam
    and the heat from their bodies
forcing exotic plants
    from stones and loam:

lobelia
    nasturtium
             wintersweet
rhubarb and garlic
    privet and night-scented stock
and somewhere behind it all
    the children they were
sailing through the dark
    on winter nights
to needle-falls and cream
    and the blood-fruit they prized
above all others:
    crimson
mythical.

The angel bound
    and stilled
in Euclid or Fibonacci
    the unprovable
fact of the physical world
and data that exist
    beyond all doubt:
sunfish
    and blue-stemmed grasses
the tender
    improbable gold
of cottonwood
    the thoughts of others
music in the dark
    the ultrasound
of bats around a pool
continuous
    with sunlight on the firth
the streaming roads
    to Perth or Invercarse
birchwoods
    and miles of pasture in the rain
come to a vivid standstill.
The fact of endurance
    decay
and the fact
    of weathering
flakes of enamel
    a splinter of broken hull
gulls flickering at the shoreline
    year after year.

Nothing has been revealed
      or hidden
and yet the tide
      in certain weathers
raises these slow
      dank angels
from the sea
      and makes them visible:
a length of hemp
      a ravelled wing of oil.

So much between healing
        and mending
a lame horse cured
        with oil and wintergreen
or treacle in the oats
        to ease a cough
though mostly
        it's the tenderness between
a drayman's hands
the heat
        in a shepherd's fingers
stills the wound
and strange things come
        to those who live
by water:
fishers with cold in their veins
        or lines of salt
along the windward seams
        of mended bones
so much still to learn
        of medicine
agar or silver for wounds
        the lucid dreams
of phosphorus
        a room
of fruits in embryo
        the weight
of silences and waking
        potash
settled in tinted jars
        and dusted tubers

wrapped in a film
        of sulphur
and is it the wind
        or rainstorms
or the sea
        repairs a soul
or is it magnetic north
        that brings us true
knitting the cut flesh
        smoothing the creases
in dreams?

The medieval lull
    of inland farms
that feeling
    a man will have
as he turns from work
    and crosses a yard
the sudden awareness of heat
    or the smell of malt
from miles away
    whatever it is that remains
in the hair or the bones
    or folded inside the ribcage
like a prayer
    that sense of a blessed self
beneath the skin
    is here
in this summer noon:
    blisters of moss
and stonecrop
    on a wall
walking shadows
    blood-heat in the veins
and hanging on tented sticks
    above the crop
these hapless birds
    – part-crow
part-Hieronymus Bosch –
the bodies falling
    dripping from the twine
like tallow
    or fat

and something in the wing
        that almost
flexes against your passing.
Primitive
        as nothing else has been
for centuries:
        spilt
barley
        or the necessary stain
of sacrifice
        this breeding calm
this gaze of meat
        and bone.

ROADS

'Transcurrir es suficiente,
                    Transcurrir es quedarse.'
                                        Octavio Paz

I DRIVING TO MIRTIOTISSA

We learned to avoid the village
to drive through the olive groves
                              evading
children and dogs
                    and old men with sodden voices
calling to one another through the trees

the way we avoided noon
                        or the sickening
halt of the butcher's doorway
leaving the white-hot streets and the slide of traffic
islands of rubble
                    flashes of broken glass
oil-slicks and fruit-spills
                              the sudden
untenable light

cruising the dirt-roads and alleys
on blue afternoons
for something we almost found
again and again:

a sand-lizard perched on a rock or a clump of thorns
the fretwork between its fingers
                                the fire-coloured throat
the spiders in the gaps between the rocks
goats in the weeds
                    their slack mouths and sun-bleared eyes

73

remembering panic
                    that faint trace of shit and vanilla
that hangs in the shade.

You were reading a book about angels
the way they appear on the road to the unsuspecting
wingless
            yet ringed with light
                                they could pass
for locals:
            men in boots and cotton shirts
a girl in a printed dress
                    beside a well

and though we imagined
we couldn't believe in such things
if anything was there
                    in that black light
we knew it would be lost
                        in no man's land

on back-roads scabbed with weeds or veiled with sand
running through chicken farms and unmapped towns
or rising to the chill
of native pine:

angels
    or Pan
– that god of sudden absence
come from the shadows to meet you
                                a hairsbreadth away
a blackness in the everyday event
like something tethered

a flock of birds descending on the church
a spill of figs
                    the unexpected chill
of spice-haunted wells
or miles of cicadas
                    stopped
in the noontime lull

though we guessed that the angel of roads
or the panic of standstills
was less than the weight of ourselves
being lost or found
                    and even this a story
                                        like

II KIDNAPPED

that story of our exile in the hills
months of pursuit
                    the roads whiting out in the dark
fresh disappearances
                    spotting the matted grass

— *they were still on my scent*
though I'd crossed those mountain streams
a dozen times

the water filling my boots
the year-long cold
seeping through my bones to fledge the groin

and I'm travelling still: my name on a borrowed passport
sleeping between the graves in an upland church
foraging for eggs and spills of grain

living caesura, less than the sum of my parts
I'm waiting for the limbo of a life
that goes without saying:

a circle in the woods of mint and coal
where someone has stopped before now
to light a fire

                  — almost
but not quite right:
illusion
          like the one who stays at home
lost in the warmth of butter and cherry tea
and wanting for nothing
                              immune to the smell of fairgrounds:
illusion
          like the one who would arrive
travelling unawares
                        though clues abound:
the smell of standing water
                              barley mows
or alpine meadows glimpsed from the early train
to Brasov
          or Cluj

those upland silences that last for days
delectable mountains
                              hillsides clad with pines
and cherries
                the grey of nearness
                                        soldiers
standing in a clearing by a truck
boys from the country in jackboots
and threadbare shirts:

                  illusory

             as all these journeys are:
home after dark
        on a late bus
            or waiting alone
at the station
      the platform light
suddenly all there is for miles around

and something I almost recall
            some hunting bird
skimming low over the tracks
          and vanishing.

And even if I recognise the shape
even if something remains
         some haunting call
I know from somewhere else
           − some film or tape −
even if some local perfume drifts
towards me
      as I cross the narrow bridge
an inkling of oilseed rape
          or ripened corn
the scent of orchards
       fish−meal
          rendered bone
there's nothing here to understand or claim
nothing to grasp
       nothing to think of

as true.

    I've come this way before
        I've read the maps:

77

the dream of a shoreline
                              the delicate upland trees
delectable mountains nuzzling the rear-view mirror
houses standing open
                              doors ajar
the windows like the gaps where angels live
in old nativities
signals above a meadow
                              porch-lights and doors
as if there were something more
to be revealed.
I have driven this road too often
                              and come too far
losing the taste for home:
                              its standing warmth
the gravities and shifts
we dwell upon

                    — so when I reach the hollow of the stairs
intruder on the dream you've shifted from

I'm glad of the silence
                              glad of the distance between us
the blackness of country roads I have smuggled in
on my shirtsleeves
                    the flavour of rain
and nothingness
                    — a gap you would not house
no matter how often you turn
                              with the feel
of something at your back
                              some hirsute god
some cloven-footed wisp of the angelic

78

– though speaking for myself
                              I'd want to say
this nothing is why I am out on a starless road
learning the true extent of no man's land
the night wind threading my eyes
                              and nowhere to go.

IV IDA Y VUELTA
i.m. Octavio Paz

Remember that Alpujarran hill-town:
gusts of broom for miles then an arabic
scribble of burning bush amongst the stones?
The empty hostel where we lay awake
till morning, while a long-awaited rain
unmapped the streets, the gardens moored in smoke,
the tree-lined squares?
                              Remember the sullen
music of cicadas, sudden panic
in the still of afternoon? – the way
we almost learned to chance upon the air
the stain of something richer – how the stay
of terror is a gift for smaller fear:
that beast we conjured from the common day:
man-sized; inert; a ghost of teeth and hair.

                      – one way to say it
perhaps

        or this: how
                      leaving Frankfurt
the plane rose slowly to a wall
of thunder-cloud
                      shuddering in its bones for the moment's
pause before the stillness
of a fall

79

then lightning over fields that bled
like the pastilles of freshened colour in a school-child's
paint-box: rapeseed yellow
                              clover green
umber and terrasiena.

How terror is always shifting
                              between the glow
of home
        and the chill of departure

Yo atravesé los arcos y los puentes
Yo estaba vivo, en busca de la vida

and love is something learned
like dancing:
knowing the steps
but moving without desire
in a partner's arms

Yo estaba vivo y vi muchos fantasmas,
Todos de carne y hueso y todos ávidos

or how a life
can never quite be seen
in this measure of rain
a bruise of kisses
seeping to the bone
and waiting there
to flower as a word

Tigre, novilla, pulpo, yedra en llamas

whichever one you choose
it's all the same:

arrival; end; hibiscus; carbon; stone.

Yo estaba vivo y fui a buscar la muerte

– an algebra
          a science of goodbyes
somewhere beyond the absence implicit in grammar:

lost
    and
found.

The road
          or the town's last street
when they worked all afternoon to build
a fairground
                men in boots and cotton shirts
rigging a world of candy-floss and diesel
and setting it alight so I could dream
of running away
                becoming the competent son
you would never imagine.
How even now
                in dreams I have failed to confess
I stand at the edge of the woods on Fulford Road
my mind on the blue of elsewhere:
                                frog-headed
vagrant
I walk to the last fuzzed streetlamp and hitch a ride
running away to the promise of freight cars in sidings
gulf-water
          wood-stoves
                disappearances.

This dream recurs
                I find it in our bed
the taste of doorways
                        windows
                                exit roads
or how there are times
                coming home
when everything seems richer for my absence:
car parks around the airport
perfectly ordered
                the crowd at the gate
with labels or startled joy
for the newly arrived

our kitchen windows flushed with light and steam
and the flavour of cherry tea that has lingered for days
while I've been gone.

Stop moving
                and another life begins:
the motion the tide conceals
                        the caress of erosion
or how the beginning of autumn is quietly gloved
in August
the first bright
sugars turning to gold
in locust trees and false acacias.

I taste it on the windows in the dusk
of morning:
a perfume so close to travel I imagine
deer trails in the hills
                the white
hiatus of woodland tracks
                        or the sherbet fizz
of rock-salt and drifted sand
on a coastal highway.

How once
          driving back to my room
in Mountain View
I wanted to stop the car and disappear
to pull in under a cypress and slip away
venturing into the nowhere
of starlight and wind
and leaving no trace.

I've run like this for years
                    and I've returned
– the promised no one left behind a door
or tethered to a borderline of sand
and poppies.

I've wanted so many lives
                    such otherness
and so much less than anything we have:
some garden of broken stones and aquilegias
a shoal of angel fish in makeshift graves
unscheduled stops
          in no man's land
                    or Tulsa

and yet
          forgive me this:
I never really mastered coming home
skilled in that childhood-for-years of travelling light

forgive me:
          I still can't resist
the sound of a fair in the distance
                         the new-crushed grass
those sixties songs
               the heat of the machines

I still can't resist the girls on the promenade
walking the front in lipstick and brand-new hairdos
the boys from the caravan parks come out
to stand in the bars all night
                              like their father's ghosts
sullen and proud
                    and as lost in the world they inherit
as stray dogs
              or mink

and forgive me
              that I cannot leave or stay
that I'm only a moment away
                              from being unseen

forgive me
          being not the man I seem
not lost or found
                  but somewhere in between.